NBA's TOP 10
RIVALRIES

BY BRIAN HALL

→ NBA's TOP 10

SportsZone
An Imprint of Abdo Publishing
abdopublishing.com

abdopublishing.com

Published by Abdo Publishing, a division of ABDO, PO Box 398166, Minneapolis, Minnesota 55439. Copyright © 2019 by Abdo Consulting Group, Inc. International copyrights reserved in all countries. No part of this book may be reproduced in any form without written permission from the publisher. SportsZone™ is a trademark and logo of Abdo Publishing.

Printed in the United States of America, North Mankato, Minnesota
042018
092018

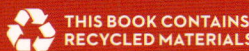
THIS BOOK CONTAINS RECYCLED MATERIALS

Cover Photo: Winslow Townson/AP Images
Interior Photos: Marcio Jose Sanchez/AP Images, 4–5; Peter Southwick/AP Images, 7; Focus On Sport/Getty Images, 9; Eric Gay/AP Images, 10; Scott Troyanos/AP Images, 11; Kathy Willens/AP Images, 13; Ron Schwane/AP Images, 14; John G. Mabanglo/European Pressphoto Agency/AP Images, 15; Ron Frehm/AP Images, 17; AP Images, 19; Mark Lennihan/AP Images, 21; Manny Millan/Sports Illustrated/Getty Images, 23; Jerry Wachter/Sports Illustrated/Getty Images, 25; Melchior DiGiacomo/Sports Illustrated/Getty Images, 26; Mark J. Terrill/AP Images, 27

Editor: Bradley Cole
Series Designer: Craig Hinton

Library of Congress Control Number: 2017962579

Publisher's Cataloging-in-Publication Data

Names: Hall, Brian, author.
Title: NBA's top 10 rivalries / by Brian Hall.
Other titles: NBA's top ten rivalries
Description: Minneapolis, Minnesota : Abdo Publishing, 2019. | Series: NBA's top 10 |Includes online resources and index.
Identifiers: ISBN 9781532114533 (lib.bdg.) | ISBN 9781532154362 (ebook)
Subjects: LCSH: Sports rivalries--United States--Juvenile literature. | Basketball--Records--United States--Juvenile literature. | Basketball--History--Juvenile literature. | National Basketball Association--Juvenile literature.
Classification: DDC 796.323--dc23

TABLE OF CONTENTS

INTRODUCTION 4

10 6
09 8
08 10
07 12
06 14
05 16
04 18
03 20
02 22
01 24

HONORABLE MENTIONS 28
GLOSSARY 30
MORE INFORMATION 31
ONLINE RESOURCES 31
INDEX 32
ABOUT THE AUTHOR 32

INTRODUCTION

Confetti rained down on the Golden State Warriors in 2017 after they won their second National Basketball Association (NBA) championship in three years. Golden State players and coaches celebrated another win over LeBron James and the Cleveland Cavaliers. The Warriors and Cavaliers had just met three straight times in the Finals. In every series, emotions ran high as each team tried to establish dominance. The Cavs and Warriors are a great example of the rivalries that have helped increase the NBA's popularity.

NBA history has been defined by rivalries. Top teams match up in the playoffs. Star players go head-to-head to push their teams forward. The biggest rivalries in the NBA develop over time. Many play out every spring in the playoffs. The animosity builds with each series as they compete to advance. An occasional punch might even be thrown as tempers flare. Here are the NBA's best rivalries.

654321

10

During their rise to power in the 1980s, the Pistons often clashed with the Celtics.

CELTICS-PISTONS

The saying goes, "If you want to be the best, you have to beat the best." One way rivalries develop is when one team is trying to take down the champions. The Boston Celtics are the ultimate NBA champions. Boston has won 17 NBA titles, the most of any team. The Celtics won three of those championships in the 1980s. Those teams featured Hall of Famers Larry Bird, Kevin McHale, Robert Parish, and Dennis Johnson. And from 1984 to 1986, the Celtics were at their best, winning two NBA titles in three years.

Other Eastern Conference teams watched with envy. The Detroit Pistons, meanwhile, were preparing to change the balance of power. Detroit was building around Hall of Fame point guard Isiah Thomas and rugged center Bill Laimbeer. The Pistons' gritty and aggressive style of play clashed with the similar no-nonsense approach of Boston.

The two teams met in the playoffs in 1985. Boston won in six games in the Eastern Conference semifinals. The rivalry escalated in Game 3 of the 1987 conference finals. Bird and Laimbeer were ejected for fighting. Laimbeer took Bird to the ground on a hard foul. The Celtics won the series in seven games. But the Pistons were getting closer.

The tables finally turned in 1988. The Pistons had given Hall of Famers Joe Dumars, Adrian Dantley, and Dennis Rodman bigger roles. They teamed with Thomas and Laimbeer to help Detroit slip past Boston in

six games in the conference finals. The Pistons then went on to win rematches in the 1989 and 1991 playoffs. It was finally Detroit's turn to be the alpha dog in the rivalry.

09

Hawks power forward Bob Pettit (9) led his team against Bill Russell, *left*, and the Celtics.

CELTICS-HAWKS

The Boston Celtics became a dynasty in the late 1950s. One key move in 1956 sent them on their way.

The St. Louis Hawks had the second overall pick in that year's NBA draft. Celtics coach Red Auerbach wanted it badly. The Hawks used the pick to draft center Bill Russell from the University of San Francisco. Then they traded him to Boston for Ed Macauley and the rights to Cliff Hagan. Both of the new Hawks would end up in the Basketball Hall of Fame. But Russell went on to basketball immortality.

The Hawks still benefited from the trade. Macauley and Hagan combined with future Hall of Famer Bob Pettit to give St. Louis a championship-caliber team. The Hawks reached the NBA Finals in 1957 and 1958. They lost to Russell and the Celtics the first time and then won a rematch the next year. But the balance clearly shifted after that.

The Hawks missed the NBA Finals in 1959, but they faced the Celtics the next two years. Boston won both times on the way to eight straight championships. No team in US sports history has had a similar string of dominance. It wasn't a bad run for St. Louis. But Hawks fans couldn't help but wonder what would have happened had they kept Russell. Perhaps the team wouldn't have moved to Atlanta in 1968, leaving St. Louis without an NBA team for more than half a century and counting.

DRAFT REGRETS

The Rochester Royals had the first pick in the 1956 NBA Draft. Instead of drafting Bill Russell, they selected guard Si Green. Their reasons for passing on Russell are disputed. In one version, Walter Brown—who owned the Celtics and was part-owner of the Ice Capades, guaranteed he'd bring the lucrative ice skating show to Rochester. Other reports said the Royals feared that Russell would sign with the Harlem Globetrotters.

The rivalry featured physical play from All-Stars Charles Barkley, *left*, and David Robinson (50).

SPURS-SUNS

The action on the basketball court was often as hot as weather in the desert Southwest when the Phoenix Suns and San Antonio Spurs met from 1992 to 2010. Even as the rosters changed, the teams seemed to always run into each other in the playoffs. The stakes were always high. And the games were usually exciting.

In the early years, forward Charles Barkley led Phoenix, while center David Robinson was the Spurs' main man. Later, point guard Steve Nash took over for the Suns and forward Tim Duncan led San Antonio.

The Western Conference was loaded in those years. No two teams met as often in the playoffs as the Suns and Spurs, who faced each other five times between 1992 and 2000. With championship hopes on the line so many times, each shove, foul, and loss made the rivalry stronger.

San Antonio and Phoenix clashed in the playoffs with championships on the line.

Phoenix swept San Antonio in the first round of the playoffs in 1992. The Suns added Barkley the next season on their way to the NBA Finals. Barkley was the league's Most Valuable Player (MVP), but first Phoenix had to get through the Spurs. The Suns won in six games in the Western Conference semifinals. Robinson, coach Gregg Popovich, and San Antonio finally beat Phoenix in 1996.

San Antonio forward Robert Horry added fire to the rivalry in 2007 when he knocked Nash into the scorer's table in Game 4 of the conference semifinals. The incident started a brawl that led to suspensions for Horry and the Suns' Amar'e Stoudemire and Boris Diaw. The Spurs won the final two games to win the series. San Antonio won five of the next six series between the teams before the Suns had the final say with a four-game sweep in 2010.

07

KNICKS-PACERS

The rivalry between the Indiana Pacers and the New York Knicks revolved around the Pacers' sharpshooting, trash-talking guard Reggie Miller. He knew just which buttons to push to rile up the Knicks and their fans. And the Knicks loved to push right back.

The tension started when Knicks guard John Starks didn't shake Miller's hand before a game. In their first playoff meeting in 1993, Miller caught Starks with an elbow in the chest. Later, after Starks made a shot, he got in Miller's face. But in the process, he head-butted Miller. Starks was ejected for the play.

A year later, the teams met again in the Eastern Conference finals. In Game 5, Miller started going at it with Knicks fan and movie director Spike Lee, who was sitting in the front row at New York's Madison Square Garden. Miller talked trash to Lee after several baskets. Lee fired comments back about the Pacers. It led to Miller staring down Lee and signaling that the Knicks would choke. Miller scored 39 points in that Game 5 victory in New York. However, the Knicks again won the series.

Miller and the Pacers finally came out on top in 1995, winning Game 7 of the Eastern Conference semifinals in New York 97–95. But the Pacers wouldn't have made it to Game 7 if not for a stunning performance by Miller in Game 1. Indiana trailed by six points with 18.7 seconds left in the game. Miller hit a three-pointer over Starks. Then Miller stole the

12

Pacers guard Reggie Miller shoots over John Starks in the 1994 playoffs.

inbounds pass and hurried behind the three-point line for another basket to tie the game. Then Miller added a pair of free throws. Eight points in nine seconds lifted the Pacers to the win. It's a great reason why the *New York Times* dubbed Miller the "Knick Killer."

The Cavs and Warriors met three years in a row with the NBA championship on the line.

CAVALIERS-WARRIORS

The Golden State Warriors and the Cleveland Cavaliers met in the 2015 NBA Finals. A parade of superstars ensured that they would meet again the next year and the year after. In fact, they became the first teams to meet in the NBA Finals in three straight years.

The Warriors stormed onto the scene with a fast-paced offense, powered by a barrage of three-point shots from the talented duo of guards Stephen Curry and Klay Thompson. The "Splash Brothers" were one of the top shooting duos in NBA history.

On the other side was LeBron James. Most had considered him to be the best player in the league for almost a decade. And he certainly was Cleveland's best player in 2015. The dynamic forward had to battle the Warriors nearly by himself. Cavaliers forward Kevin Love was out of

LeBron James, Draymond Green, *center*, and Kevin Durant demonstrate that rivalries can get heated in the playoffs.

the playoffs with an injury. Then point guard Kyrie Irving went down in Game 1. Golden State won the series in six games.

The Warriors looked like they were going to cruise to another title the following year. Golden State had won a record 73 games. Then the Warriors took a 3–1 lead in the Finals. But James was determined. No Cleveland sports team had won a major league championship since the 1960s. He made sure that changed. James made history when he scored 41 points in back-to-back games as the Cavaliers tied the series.

Game 7 was tied late when James streaked across the court to swat away a layup attempt by Golden State guard Andre Iguodala. The play became one of the most famous in NBA history. Cleveland finally won, and James was named the Finals MVP. The Cavaliers became the first team in NBA history to win after trailing 3–1 in the Finals. The loss was deflating for Golden State. So they went out and got even better.

That summer Golden State signed 2014 NBA MVP Kevin Durant away from Oklahoma City. Durant joined fellow league MVP Curry, turning Golden State into a so-called "superteam." The Warriors met expectations by beating James and Cleveland in the Finals in five games.

05

Michael Jordan returned from retirement with a statement game against the Knicks.

BULLS-KNICKS

One-sided rivalries make the losing teams angry and upset. Winning teams brush off the losers like pesky, annoying bugs. It was this way for the New York Knicks whenever they faced the Chicago Bulls. The rivals seemed to meet in the Eastern Conference playoffs every year in the 1990s. And just about every time, the Bulls won.

It was especially unfortunate timing for Knicks Hall of Fame center Patrick Ewing. He had the bad luck of playing in the East at the same time as Michael Jordan.

Jordan's Bulls won six NBA championships in an eight-year span. New York was a frequent roadblock along the way. The Bulls and the Knicks faced off six times in the playoffs from 1989 to 1996. Five times the Bulls ended the Knicks' playoff hopes. New York's only series victory was in the 1994 Eastern Conference semifinals, when Jordan was away playing baseball.

Jordan led Chicago to its first three NBA titles from 1991 to 1993. The Bulls went through the Knicks each year. New York advanced to the NBA Finals when Jordan was playing baseball, but the rivalry wasn't over.

Jordan returned to Chicago in 1995 and showed he'd shaken off the rust in his fifth game back in New York's Madison Square Garden. Jordan scored 55 points as he made a defensively stout Knicks team look silly.

JORDAN'S FAVORITE DUNK

Michael Jordan has said his favorite dunk of all time came against the Knicks in the 1991 playoffs. He was double-teamed near the baseline before spinning free and then dunking over a leaping Patrick Ewing.

The game is remembered as the "double-nickel" game. Jordan and the Bulls then left the Knicks in the dust a year later in the playoffs on their way to Chicago's second "three-peat."

04

CELTICS-76ERS

The Boston Celtics and Syracuse Nationals rivalry started like a lot of Boston's rivalries. The Nationals challenged Boston's early dominance in the NBA. They beat the Celtics in three out of seven playoff series between 1953 and 1961. The rivalry took a big step in 1963 when Syracuse moved to Philadelphia and became the 76ers.

Center Wilt Chamberlain returned to Philadelphia to join the Sixers in 1965. By that time, center Bill Russell was leading the Celtics to annual championships. The matchups between the two dominant centers only made the rivalry more exciting.

Chamberlain and Russell had clashing styles. Chamberlain was a physically dominant player with outstanding scoring abilities. Russell was a spectacular defensive player who made his many excellent teammates even better. Chamberlain and Russell faced off in the playoffs four straight years. Boston won three of the four series. The Celtics added another win against Philadelphia in 1969, a year after Chamberlain was traded to the Los Angeles Lakers.

After Russell's retirement in 1969, both teams faded and the rivalry fizzled. But the competition heated up again in 1976. Philadelphia purchased Hall of Famer Julius Erving from the New York Nets that year. The teams then met in the 1977 playoffs, with Philadelphia winning. The Celtics drafted forward Larry Bird a year later. The rivalry thrived with

Bill Russell (6) went head to head with Wilt Chamberlain on both ends of the court.

Bird and Erving, another set of clashing styles. Erving was the high-flying "Dr. J," known for his breathtaking dunks. Bird's deadly shooting and no-look passes set the tone for an exciting Celtics squad.

The teams met in the Eastern Conference finals four times between 1980 and 1985. Each team won two series, and the games were split 12–12. A 1983 exhibition game between the teams turned ugly. Celtics forward Cedric Maxwell threw the ball at the head of 76ers center Moses Malone. Maxwell and Malone fought. Bird and Sixers forward Marc Iavaroni had an altercation. Boston's Gerald Henderson also threw a punch at Philadelphia's Sedale Threatt. Even when the games didn't count, these were two teams that didn't like each other.

03

Jeff Van Gundy, *bottom*, tries to break up a fight between Alonzo Mourning (33) and Charles Oakley.

HEAT-KNICKS

A rivalry triggered by a coach changing sides became one of the NBA's meanest matchups. Pat Riley was the head coach of the New York Knicks. But he left in 1995 over a contract dispute and became president and coach of the Miami Heat. The Knicks filed tampering charges against Miami, and the Heat ended up surrendering $1 million and a draft pick to New York. The move created bad blood between the Knicks and Heat off the court.

The rivalry was turned up a notch when the Heat acquired All-Star center Alonzo Mourning. Mourning already didn't like Knicks forward Larry Johnson from their days as teammates in the early '90s with the Charlotte Hornets. The fresh rivalry only made these tensions worse.

The teams met in the second round of the 1997 playoffs. In Game 5, Miami forward P. J. Brown flipped Knicks guard Charlie Ward over his head and the Knicks bench emptied. Ward, Johnson, Patrick Ewing, John Starks, and Allan Houston were suspended. Brown was suspended for two games. The Heat trailed in the series 3–1 before the fight, but with the help of the suspensions, Miami prevailed in seven games.

The most famous encounter was in Game 4 of their first-round series in 1998. Mourning and Johnson began throwing punches at each other, and a brawl started. Knicks coach Jeff Van Gundy wound up grabbing Mourning's leg to try to break up the fight. The 5-foot-9-inch Van Gundy

slipped to the ground clutching Mourning's knee while the 7-footer swung at Knicks forward Charles Oakley.

    The Knicks and Heat met in the playoffs for four straight years, from 1997 to 2000. After the Heat won the first series, New York won the last three, getting the last laugh on Riley.

02

The Pistons and Bulls battled for supremacy of the Central Division and the NBA.

BULLS-PISTONS

The Eastern Conference witnessed the rise and fall of three powers in the 1980s and early 1990s. Boston's window was closing as Detroit won back-to-back titles in 1989 and 1990. Then the Pistons' reign ended at the hands of Michael Jordan and the Bulls.

Detroit had to contend with Chicago's emerging dynasty while trying to establish its own dominance. Chicago and Detroit met in the playoffs four straight years. The Pistons won the first three encounters while on their way to three straight NBA Finals from 1988 to 1990.

The losses were deflating for the Bulls. If Jordan was to prove he was the superstar many thought he could be, he would have to get his team past the bruising Pistons. And he finally did in a four-game sweep in 1991.

The Pistons were known as the "Bad Boys" for their physical play, and there was plenty of hostility between the rivals. The Pistons famously walked off the court after the series-deciding game in 1991 without shaking hands with Chicago's players.

The heart of the rivalry was the feud between Jordan and Pistons point guard Isiah Thomas. Thomas grew up in Chicago. But his hometown fans came to embrace his rival, Jordan. Thomas was accused of "freezing out" Jordan in the 1985 All-Star Game. Jordan took just nine shots in the game.

JORDAN RULES

Detroit came up with the so-called "Jordan Rules" in an attempt to slow down the Chicago superstar. Joe Dumars was responsible for defending Michael Jordan. But the rest of the Bad Boys helped by getting physical with Jordan whenever possible.

Thomas later denied the freeze-out occurred. However, Jordan and Bulls teammate Scottie Pippen were thought to be instrumental in Thomas's absence from the 1992 Dream Team Olympic basketball lineup.

01

Earvin "Magic" Johnson and Larry Bird were key figures in this legendary rivalry.

CELTICS-LAKERS

There's little doubt that the most iconic rivalry in NBA history belongs to the Celtics and Lakers. When two teams are great through several eras and feature many competitive matchups with championships in the balance, rivalry is sure to follow. The rivalry has played out in four different decades. The teams faced each other in a record 12 NBA Finals through 2018, with Boston winning nine. However, the Lakers had won three of the past four.

The Celtics and Lakers clearly are NBA royalty. Boston owns 17 NBA titles. The Lakers have 16 championships over their franchise history, from Minneapolis to Los Angeles. They have combined to win nearly half of all NBA titles.

The rivalry has also featured some of the best individual matchups in the game's history. Centers Bill Russell and Wilt Chamberlain continued their rivalry when Chamberlain was traded to Los Angeles. Bird and Earvin "Magic" Johnson brought their rivalry from college to the NBA. Kobe Bryant and Paul Pierce were two of the more recent stars.

The Celtics became an NBA powerhouse with eight straight championships starting in 1959. That streak of titles is the most by any team in US professional sports. Boston won its first championship of the stretch against the Minneapolis Lakers. They won four more against the Lakers after the franchise moved to Los Angeles in 1960.

Russell led the Celtics in the early years of the rivalry with fellow Hall of Famers Tommy Heinsohn, John Havlicek, and Sam Jones by his side. Hall of Famers Elgin Baylor, Jerry West, and Gail Goodrich played for the Lakers before Chamberlain joined the rivalry in 1968. In all, 12 Hall of Famers played in the rivalry during the 1960s.

Bird and Magic took the competition—and the NBA—to another level. The NBA's popularity nationally grew as the two stars added their own spin on the rivalry. They offered two contrasting styles. There was Bird and the Celtics' blue-collar ethic. Johnson and the Lakers were nicknamed "Showtime" for their flair and Hollywood style. The rivalry was reflected by the teams' fans as well. Much of the nation could find a way to identify with one of the two teams.

Boston and Los Angeles faced off in the finals three times in the 1980s. Bird and the Celtics won in 1984. One memorable encounter included Boston forward Kevin McHale taking down Lakers forward Kurt Rambis and starting a scuffle. Johnson and the Lakers came back and won in 1985. Los Angeles would beat Boston one more time in 1987.

Years passed before Bryant and Pierce reignited the rivalry in 2008. Boston added Kevin Garnett and Ray Allen in trades to join Pierce. Bryant and the Lakers won three straight NBA titles but had lost Hall of Fame center Shaquille O'Neal. Los Angeles traded for Pau Gasol to give Bryant another big man to play with.

The Celtics' stars beat the Lakers in 2008.

Wilt Chamberlain, *left*, and Jerry West work a two-man game on Boston's John Havlicek.

26

SPOILING FRIENDSHIP

Intense matchups between Wilt Chamberlain and Bill Russell didn't stop the two big men from being friends. The rivalry finally got to them, though. Russell accused Chamberlain of faking an injury in the 1969 series. Chamberlain didn't like the accusation, and the two didn't speak for 20 years.

Kobe Bryant and Paul Pierce met twice in the NBA Finals as the rivalry continued to burn.

Bryant and Gasol flipped the result two years later with Bryant's fifth title. With so many big wins, big losses, and NBA championships on the line, the rivalry has stood the test of time.

HONORABLE MENTIONS

KINGS-LAKERS: Northern California against Southern California was just a small part of this rivalry, which burned brightest in the early 2000s. Los Angeles center Shaquille O'Neal called Sacramento the "Queens." There was also the famous fight between Lakers forward Rick Fox and Kings guard Doug Christie to demonstrate the dislike in two testy playoff series in back-to-back seasons.

LAKERS-SUNS: Kobe Bryant once said that he considered Phoenix to be his biggest rival. Steve Nash and the Suns eliminated Bryant and the Lakers from the playoffs in 2006 and 2007.

LAKERS-SPURS: The Lakers and the Spurs were the best teams in the Western Conference during the late 1990s and 2000s. Either San Antonio or Los Angeles represented the West in the NBA Finals in 11 of 12 seasons between 1999 and 2010. The road to the finals often included a matchup between the two. Kobe Bryant and Spurs center Tim Duncan were the key players.

THUNDER-WARRIORS: A budding rivalry began after Kevin Durant left Oklahoma City to join Golden State. Their meetings have been intense, with Thunder star Russell Westbrook seeming to take Durant's move personally.

LAKERS-PISTONS: Each team was trying to establish its dominance and also trying to get past Boston in the 1980s. Los Angeles and Detroit met in two straight NBA Finals. The Lakers won in 1988 with the Pistons taking the crown in 1989. The rivalry also soured the friendship of Magic Johnson and Isiah Thomas.

HEAT-SPURS: This rivalry is almost player-versus-team. LeBron James ran into San Antonio in the NBA Finals three times. The Spurs denied James a championship in 2007 when he played for Cleveland. James signed with Miami and faced San Antonio in the finals in back-to-back seasons. James and the Heat won in 2013. The Spurs came back and won in 2014.

GLOSSARY

BARRAGE
A concentrated outpouring.

DRAFT
A system that allows teams to acquire new players coming into a league.

DYNAMIC
Positive in attitude and full of energy and new ideas.

DYNASTY
A team that has an extended period of success, usually winning multiple championships in the process.

REIGN
Ruling over a team or league.

ROSTER
A list of players on a team.

RUGGED
Tough and determined.

SUPREMACY
Being the best over a period of time.

TAMPERING
Illegally contacting a player or coach who is under contract with another team.

MORE INFORMATION

ONLINE RESOURCES

To learn more about famous NBA rivalries, visit **abdobooklinks.com**. These links are routinely monitored and updated to provide the most current information available.

BOOKS

Ervin, Phil. *Total Basketball*. Minneapolis, MN: Abdo Publishing, 2017.

Graves, Will. *Make Me the Best Basketball Player*. Minneapolis, MN: Abdo Publishing, 2017.

Silverman, Drew. *The NBA Finals*. Minneapolis, MN: Abdo Publishing, 2013.

PLACE TO VISIT

NAISMITH MEMORIAL BASKETBALL HALL OF FAME
1000 Hall of Fame Avenue
Springfield, MA 01105
413-781-6500
hoophall.com

The Basketball Hall of Fame is like a museum dedicated to basketball. It highlights the greatest players, coaches, and moments in the sport's history. Many of the players mentioned in this book are enshrined there. It is home to more than 300 inductees and more than 40,000 square feet of basketball history.

INDEX

Barkley, Charles, 10–11
Bird, Larry, 6, 18–19, 24, 26
Bryant, Kobe, 24, 26–27

Chamberlain, Wilt, 18, 24–25, 27
Curry, Stephen, 14–15

Dumars, Joe, 6, 23
Durant, Kevin, 15

Erving, Julius, 18–19
Ewing, Patrick, 16, 17, 20

Havlicek, John, 25
Heinsohn, Tommy, 25
Houston, Allan, 20

Iguodala, Andre, 15
Irving, Kyrie, 15

James, LeBron, 4, 14–15
Johnson, Larry, 20
Johnson, Magic, 24, 26
Jordan, Michael, 16–17, 22–23

Laimbeer, Bill, 6
Lee, Spike, 12
Love, Kevin, 14

Malone, Moses, 19
McHale, Kevin, 6, 26
Miller, Reggie, 12–13
Mourning, Alonzo, 20–21

Pettit, Bob, 8
Pierce, Paul, 24, 26
Pippen, Scottie, 23
Popovich, Gregg, 11

Rambis, Kurt, 26
Riley, Pat, 20–21
Robinson, David, 10–11
Russell, Bill, 8, 9, 18, 24–25, 27

Starks, John, 12, 20
Stoudemire, Amar'e, 11

Thomas, Isiah, 6, 22–23
Thompson, Klay, 14

ABOUT THE AUTHOR

Brian Hall has been a reporter in Minnesota for more than a decade, covering a variety of sports. From Adrian Peterson to Joe Mauer, and Zach Parise to Kevin Garnett, he has interviewed and written about some of the biggest names in Minnesota sports. He currently lives in Minnesota with his wife and two sons.